I Can Show You I Care

Compassionate Touch for Children

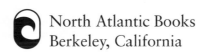

To
Natalie –
You are
changing this world
in magnificent ways!
♡ Sue Cotta

Susan Cotta

illustrations by Gregory Crawford

North Atlantic Books
Berkeley, California

UI Enterprises
Palm Beach Gardens, Florida

One day Patrick and his dog Clarence were playing hide-and-go-seek in their backyard. His father was busy raking leaves. Patrick couldn't wait to jump into the pile.

As Patrick was running, he fell over
a tree root and bumped his knee.
He started to cry. His knee really hurt!

"Are you OK, Patrick?"

"My knee hurts a lot, Dad!"

Patrick's dad gently put his hands around his knee. "Your knee's going to be all right."

It felt good to have his father's hands on his knee. His dad's eyes were closed. Patrick breathed deeply, and closed his eyes, too.

"Dad, what's happening?" asked Patrick. "It's getting warm. It's feeling better."

Dad smiled. "My mom did this for me when I hurt myself. Her caring thoughts came through her hands and took the pain away."

"I'm bringing warmth, like sunshine,
through my hands and into your knee!
These days it's called Compassionate Touch."

"Can I do it, too?" Patrick asked.

'Sure. Anyone can!" His father ruffled his hair. "Make sure it's okay first, then put your hands either on or near the hurt place, and think good thoughts. Maybe like playing with Clarence, or a bright rainbow of colors — anything that makes you happy."

'You mean like horses running in the wind?" asked Patrick.

'You got it!" said his father.

That night Patrick remembered what his dad had done to his knee. It had felt good.

Maybe he could help when his friends got hurt—like when Billy pushed Cassandra down at recess last week.

On the way home Billy and his tough friends had chased Patrick and Rafael on their bikes, taunting them. "Ha, Ha, Rafael can't read. He's a DUMMY!" they yelled. It was scary.

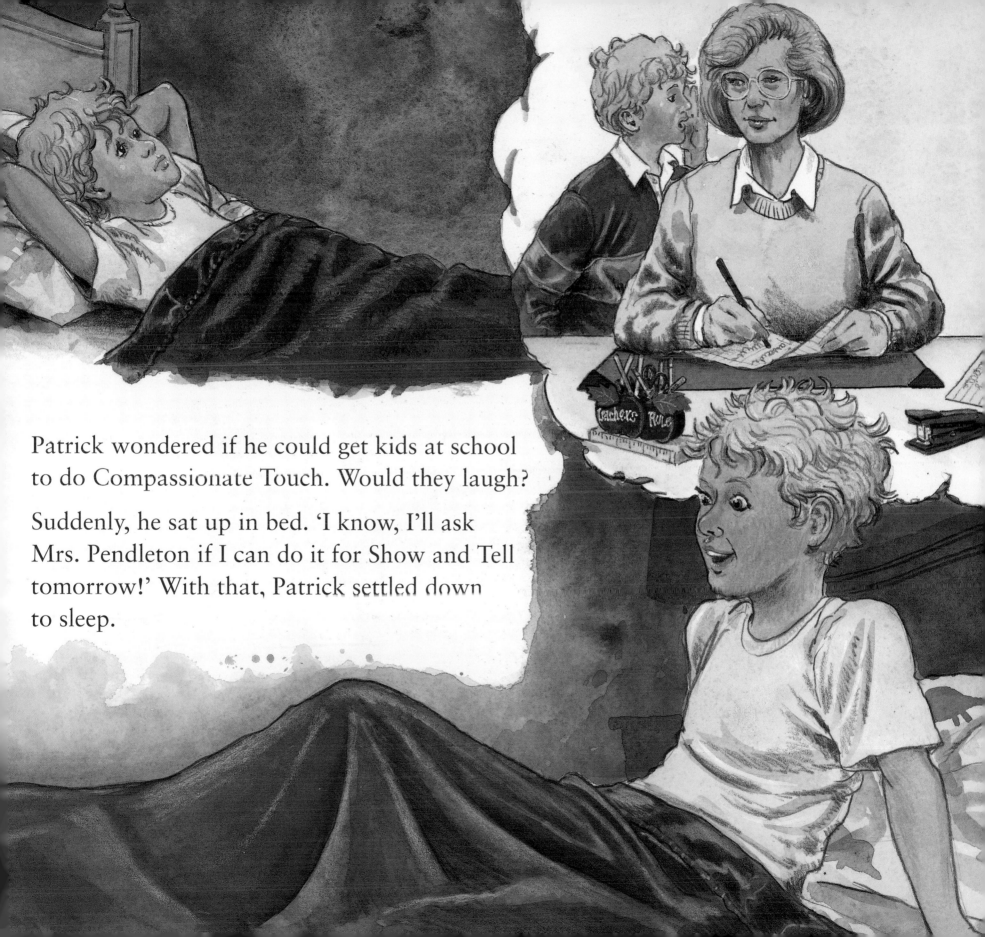

Patrick wondered if he could get kids at school to do Compassionate Touch. Would they laugh?

Suddenly, he sat up in bed. 'I know, I'll ask Mrs. Pendleton if I can do it for Show and Tell tomorrow!' With that, Patrick settled down to sleep.

telephone
telegraph
lau_gh

Assembly at
4th period

The next day, Patrick couldn't wait for Show and Tell. When Mrs. Pendleton called the children into their circle, Patrick stood proudly by her side with Rafael.

"Patrick has something very special to share with us today," said Mrs. Pendleton. "Let's be good listeners."

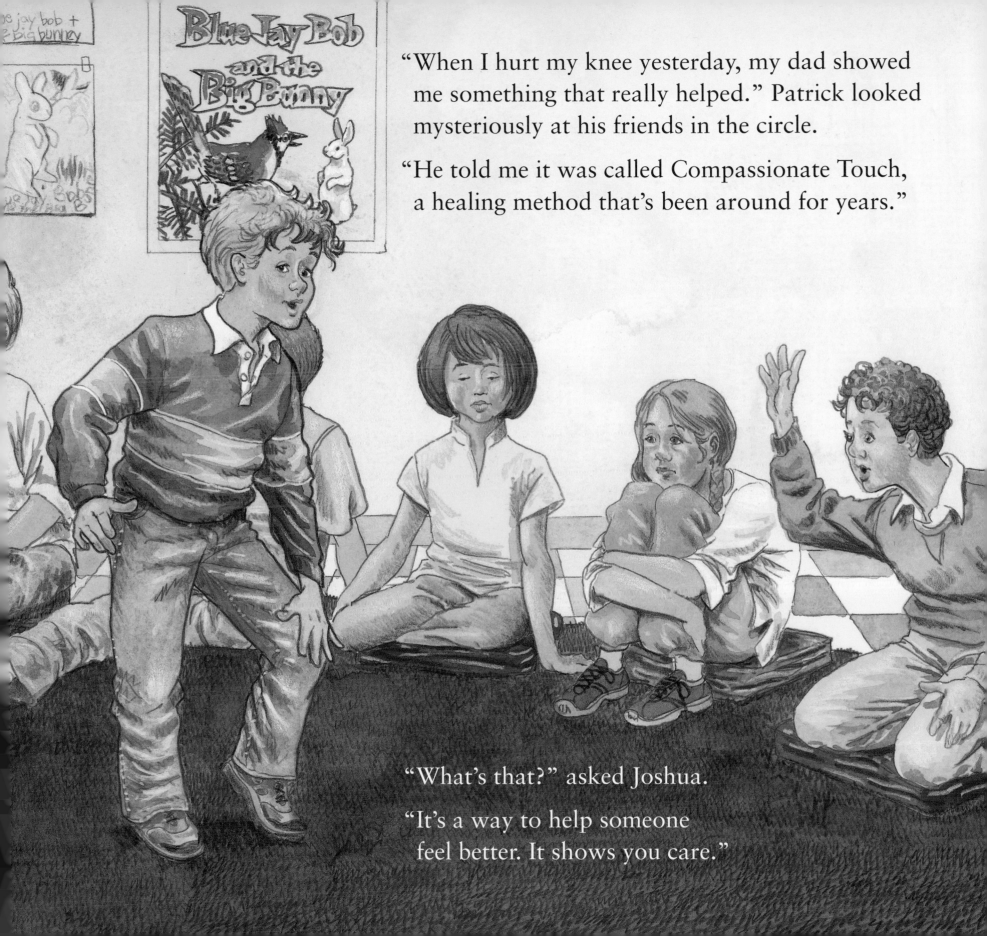

"When I hurt my knee yesterday, my dad showed me something that really helped." Patrick looked mysteriously at his friends in the circle.

"He told me it was called Compassionate Touch, a healing method that's been around for years."

"What's that?" asked Joshua.

"It's a way to help someone feel better. It shows you care."

"You put your hands on or near the hurt place and think positive thoughts. This creates energy which you can let flow into your hands. It's awesome! The spot gets really warm."

"If Rafael hurt his knee,
I could put my hands
like this ... on his knee."

"Or like this."

"Or if it hurt too much for me to put them
directly *on* his knee, I could hold them above."

"Why would we do this?" asked Billy. "I think it's dumb. I don't want to touch anybody."

Mrs. Pendleton smiled patiently, "Sometimes people get hurt. We want to help, but we don't know what to do."

"That's right!" said Aimee. "Sometimes I don't know how to help when things go wrong or someone falls down."

"I hurt my hand playing baseball yesterday," said José. "No one even noticed."

"Yesterday, Cassandra hurt her elbow when Billy pushed her down," said Kathryn.

"She was in my way!" snapped Billy.

"All right children, we dealt with that yesterday."

COMPASSIONATE TOUCH
- Kindness
- Caring
- Respect

"That's one kind of hurt, a physical one. Can you think of any other ways we feel hurt?" asked Mrs. Pendleton.

Zachary raised his hand. "No one ever lets me play dodge ball. That hurts my feelings."

"Yes, our feelings get hurt," Mrs. Pendleton said. "We want to show we care when someone is hurting on the inside or on the outside."

"Anyone want to try?" asked Mrs. Pendleton. She could hear her class beginning to get excited.

Allie shouted, "I'll try it!"

"Me, too!" said Mandy.

Dawn and Zachary chimed, "Me, too! Me, too!"

Gail and Joshua were already trying out Compassionate Touch on each other.

Mrs. Pendleton quieted her class. She paired up the boys and girls. "Let's all put both hands around your partner's elbow. Bring the energy from your thoughts into your hands. You might even want to close your eyes to concentrate." The room became very still as they worked.

"I can feel my elbow heating up!" exclaimed Joshua.

"My hands are starting to buzz," said Gail.

"Yeah! That's what I felt when my dad held my knee," Patrick said.

After a while, Mrs. Pendleton called them together again. "Boys and girls, you did a great job! If you were the giver, what kinds of things did you imagine?"

"I brought a rainbow from the sky into my hands," said Mandy.

"I have an idea. Let's do a class project on Compassionate Touch," said Mrs. Pendleton.

For the rest of the afternoon, the class cut out hands and figures.

COMPASSIONATE TOUCH
Kindness · Caring · Respect

The next day, Mrs. Pendleton was all smiles as she stood in front of their brand new bulletin board. "Now," she said, "don't forget: Every time you show you care by doing an act of Compassionate Touch, choose a cutout and stick it anywhere on this bulletin board. Let's see how many different people we can affect with Compassionate Touch."

During recess, Billy angrily yelled at Kathryn. "You tattletale! Why'd you have to get me in trouble again! You're mean! I hate you!" Billy stomped over to his friends and glared at her.

Kathryn started crying. Patrick and Rafael walked over. "Is it okay if we do Compassionate Touch on you?" Patrick asked softly.

"Okay," Kathryn sniffled. They put their hands on her shoulders.

Kathryn took a deep breath and stopped crying. Slowly, she started to feel better. Her shoulders were feeling warm.

"Thanks, guys, that really helped!"

Patrick and Rafael were very proud to be the first ones to stick their helping hands on the bulletin board.

On their way home, Cassandra and Allie noticed Billy and his friends playing baseball. All of a sudden, SMACK! Billy got hit on his wrist by a fastball. "OW!" he yelled. Billy grabbed his wrist and fell to the ground. The game stopped. No one knew what to do.

"Come on Allie," said Cassandra. "Let's help Billy."

"Billy? Why should we help him?"

"You know . . . our class project, Allie! Compassionate Touch!

"All right . . . but you have to do it," Allie said reluctantly.

Cassandra approached Billy, who was still on the ground. He was crying.

"I can help you Billy, if you'll let me."

Billy shrugged. Cassandra reached down and held Billy's wrist.

After awhile, Billy started to move his wrist. It felt pretty good. He looked up at Cassandra. "Thanks," he said grudgingly.

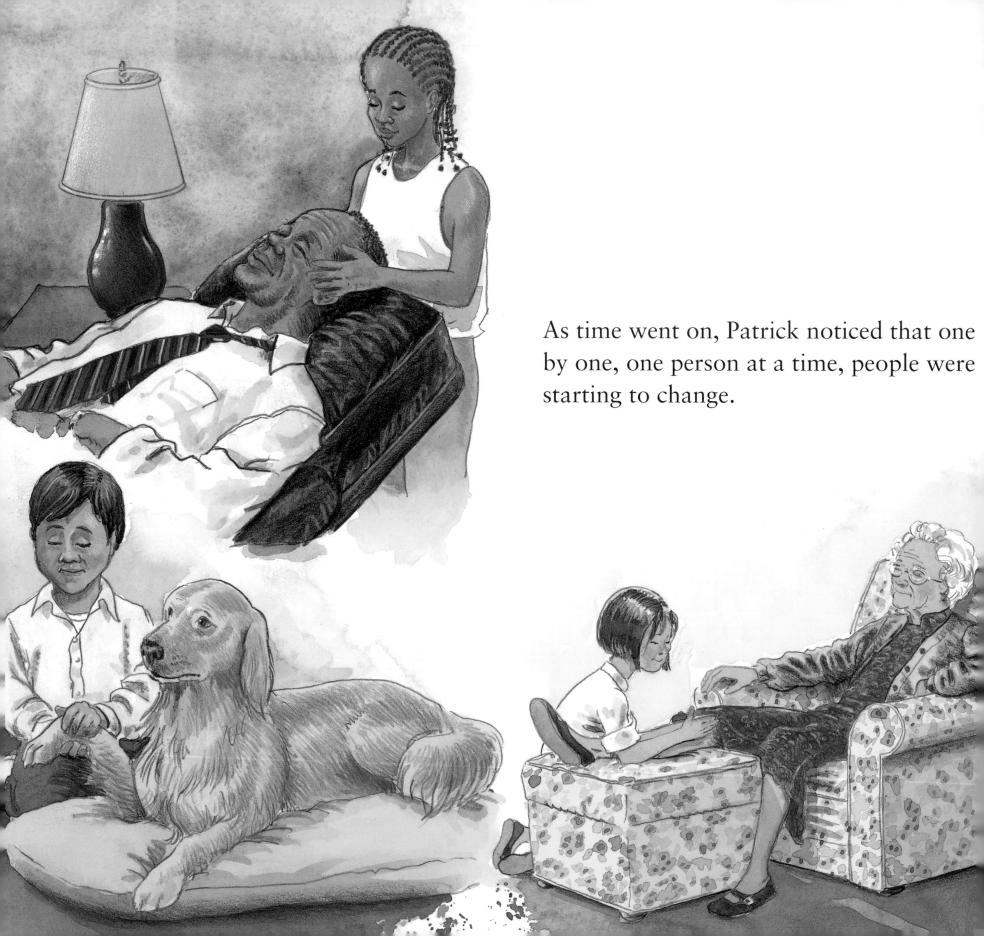

As time went on, Patrick noticed that one by one, one person at a time, people were starting to change.

Over the next few weeks, Mrs. Pendelton felt a different mood in the classroom.

When Kathryn's pencil broke, Rafael got her another.

Gail had a nosebleed during reading circle and Mandy brought her the Kleenex box.

What a better place this classroom is becoming, Mrs. Pendleton thought to herself.

A month later, at the end of the day, Billy shyly walked up to the bulletin board and placed a blue hand on it. He thought to himself, "This isn't so bad!"

Patrick saw him and was impressed. Big changes had happened in their classroom! Person by person, people were beginning to show one another empathy. What would it be like if kids all over started to show they really cared? It might change the world!

As a physical therapist, teacher, and aunt, I have seen a change in the world of children. They see more violence, inequities, biases, poverty, and despair than previous generations of children.

This book attempts to give children a sense of control and hope by empowering them with a simple act of kindness: gentle touch — a safe, compassionate touch. This touch, innate to many of us, has been largely ignored and even forbidden in some schools and health care settings. This lack of touch is changing children: they, like all of us, need touch to survive. This kind of touch is a key to eliminating violence in the home, schools, on the streets, and, yes, in the world.

The Upledger Institute has begun a pilot program for K-6 schools in Compassionate Touch. They have documented that children who are taught and encouraged to show empathy for one another show a significant decrease in problem behaviors, as well as an increase in pro-social behavior within just a three-month period.

I Can Show You I Care: Compassionate Touch for Children is a book about fostering safe, healthy touch. It is my belief and hope that changing one person at a time will make the world a better place to live.

—Susan Cotta

If you would like to start a program in
Compassionate Touch at a local school, contact:
Barbara Richmond
The Compassionate Touch Program
The Upledger Institute
11211 Prosperity Farms Road, D-325
Palm Beach Gardens, FL 33410-3487
(800) 233-5880 x 1315
E-mail: barbara@upledger.com

North Atlantic Books' publications are available through most bookstores. For further information, call 800-337-2665 or visit our website at www.northatlanticbooks.com.

Substantial discounts on bulk quantities are available to corporations, professional associations, and other organizations. For details and discount information, contact our special sales department.

Published by
North Atlantic Books
P.O. Box 12327
Berkeley, California 94712

and

UI Enterprises
11211 Prosperity Farms Road, Ste. D-325
Palm Beach Gardens, Florida 33410

ISBN 1-55643-433-2
Library of Congress Catalog Card Number 2003007249

Cover and book design by Jennifer Dunn
Distributed to the book trade by Publishers Group West
Printed in Singapore

I Can Show You I Care: Compassionate Touch for Children is sponsored by the Society for the Study of Native Arts and Sciences, a nonprofit educational corporation whose goals are to develop an educational and crosscultural perspective linking various scientific, social, and artistic fields; to nurture a holistic view of arts, sciences, humanities, and healing; and to publish and distribute literature on the relationship of mind, body, and nature.

2 3 4 5 6 7 8 9 TWP 12 11 10 09 08 07 06